Wisdoms and Inspirations

Carrie Karpoff

Copyright © 2016 Carrie Karpoff.

Interior Photography and Artwork Credit: Carrie Karpoff

Author photo by Denise Smith

All rights reserved. No part of this book may be reproduced, stored, or transmitted by any means—whether auditory, graphic, mechanical, or electronic—without written permission of both publisher and author, except in the case of brief excerpts used in critical articles and reviews. Unauthorized reproduction of any part of this work is illegal and is punishable by law.

ISBN: 978-0-9950-3830-1 (sc)
ISBN: 978-0-9950-3831-8 (e)

Library of Congress Control Number: 2016904686

Because of the dynamic nature of the Internet, any web addresses or links contained in this book may have changed since publication and may no longer be valid. The views expressed in this work are solely those of the author and do not necessarily reflect the views of the publisher, and the publisher hereby disclaims any responsibility for them.

Sunnyday Publishing rev. date: 04/25/2016

Dedication

To my husband, Al: I thank you for all the love and support you have given me over the years, especially during my journey back into the art world and in writing this book. Thank you for sharing your life with me. Thank you for being my best friend. I love you.

To Thyra Whitford: Without your guidance and enlightenment, this book may not have been written. I had no plan to write a book—and here I was writing one! You have inspired me time and time again—to grab some paper and draw, to get a canvas and paint, and to be patient and loving with myself and others. Your belief in me and your teachings over the years have allowed me to believe in myself and search for my higher purpose.

To my mom, who lived her life graciously and who loved unconditionally. By her example, she taught me about love and generosity. She will forever inspire me. The thought of her smile will always brighten my day.

To my family and friends with whom I've been given the gift of time. Although you aren't named specifically here, please know the impact you have had in my life. In our lives, we have experienced feelings of love, disappointment, happiness, and sadness together. We have been there for each other to face the challenges life has thrown our way. Thank you.

Through these experiences, I have learned and continue to learn.

Thank you for being with me on this journey. I am truly blessed.

Preface

There are many beautiful writers and inspirational leaders who provide us with words of wisdom and guidance. I was guided to write this book so I could share my perspective on the inspiration and wisdom I continue to learn and work on. These human issues are not unique to me; I realize that someone else may benefit from my perspective on these teachings.

Part of the learning process is recognizing the lessons of our past, the opportunities in our present, and how those opportunities can be transformed into a more fulfilling and joyful future. We can make a difference; we all have the ability. Life is a precious gift. Our planet and all who reside here are precious gifts as well. It is our responsibility to take care of ourselves and each other.

We're all on a journey that is leading and teaching us to become more spiritually evolved human beings. There is so much we can learn from each other, as well as from animals and the symbolism within nature. We just need to listen and look. It's important we acknowledge and respect all with whom we co-exist.

It is my hope that you find something within these pages that resonates within you. I hope it helps you at this time in your life.

Love resides within you;
let it radiate outward.

Lend a Hand

Interpreting animal symbolism provides us with the opportunity to learn lessons that we can apply to our own lives.

The Butterfly

From the cocoon, a butterfly emerges. This beautiful creature undergoes a massive amount of transition in its short lifetime. Observing the butterfly and learning its symbolic meaning allows us the opportunity to apply it to our own life's journey.

A Symbol of Transformation and Faith

We can learn to accept the changes in our lives and keep our faith as we undergo such transitions. The butterfly is also a symbol of having a light-hearted and joyful attitude; it is a being that truly knows how to live in the moment.

You Are Enough.

Love and Honour Yourself.

Happiness is a choice you make for yourself.

The desire to be loved just as you are requires that you love others just as they are.

Any recipe for self-respect and respect of others would not be complete without these ingredients:

Kindness

~

Acceptance

~

Forgiveness

Be open and willing to forgive
yourself and others.

~

It will bring healing and peace.

Nourish:

Mind,

Body,

Soul,

and

Spirit.

Just as we can gain wisdom from interpreting animal symbolism, a similar regard for and study of nature holds information and lessons that can be applied to our own lives.

The Birch Tree

From the soil stands the birch tree, tall and strong. It is considered sacred in many cultures for its adaptability, strength, and protection.

A Symbol of Renewal, Stability, and Healing

The birch tree has symbolic significance in both modern culture and mythological traditions. A highly adaptive being, it has earned its symbolic meaning of renewal through its ability to repopulate.

The birch tree has graciously shared herself to provide so much: shelter; bark for paper; sap that can be made into a refreshing drink; leaves that can be infused for tea; twigs that have been used in marriage ceremonies as a symbol of happiness and love.

She is strong and resilient.

The birch-tree sap also carries holistic medicinal properties; it is a wonderful tonic and detoxifier.

The birch tree is but one example of how nature shares herself with us.

The beauty of a bridge:

lies in its ability to let us see from both sides.

It stands as a reminder that even though something may appear to be the same, it can look very different from another perspective.

Be gentle with yourself.

And be gentle with the hearts of others.

What you do has impact and effect.

Find the positive

in people,

in situations,

in life.

A river is a wonderful metaphor for one's journey. It has a past, a present, and a future. It is energy. It is in motion.

Just as a river changes course along its way, you may too. Have faith that you will end up exactly where you were intended to.

Life is a journey taking us from one experience to another. Each experience provides us with knowledge to help us create our own best self.

You always have a choice.

Practice Kindness:

It's something we can all be good at.

You are unique and wonderful.

A little bending won't break you.

Remember, today is a gift!

Be someone's sunshine.

Acknowledge the blessings in your life!

Be a student of life

and then teach others.

*Remember to breathe ...
in through your nose and out
through your mouth.*

Life is a precious journey. Like all journeys, some are short and some are long. Each one is different based on the things we're here to learn and teach others.

Your journey is the only one within your control, so don't worry about anyone else's. We are not intended to do this all on our own. Ask for help and support whenever you need it. Be a support to others along the way.

May light continue to shine upon your path, keeping you on it and guiding you.

About the Author

From a young age, Carrie Karpoff has had a strong desire to help people. She has worked in both practical medicine and holistic healing. Both fields offer a service to others—that is, to help others and provide opportunities for healing.

Through study, she became a Reiki master practitioner. It is through this part of her journey that she received a deeper love and appreciation for the energy found in and around us, in people, in animals, and in nature. Carrie has combined an awakened sense of purpose and a renewed passion for art and writing with a desire to spread healing thoughts to the reader. In doing so, she seeks to remind others to acknowledge the beauty that surrounds them at any given time.

May you see beauty every day, in people, animals, and nature.
May you find inspiration that touches your soul.

www.ingramcontent.com/pod-product-compliance
Lightning Source LLC
Chambersburg PA
CBHW041833170426
43191CB00045B/42